Organizing a Youth Ministry to Fit Your Needs

Organizing a Youth Ministry to Fit Your Needs

Jeffrey D. Jones
Kenneth C. Potts

Judson Press® Valley Forge

The Scripture quotations in this publication are from the Revised Standard Version of the Bible copyrighted 1946, 1952 © 1971, 1973 by the Division of Christian Education of the National Council of the Churches of Christ in the U.S.A., and used by permission.

Library of Congress Cataloging in Publication Data

Jones, Jeffrey D.
   Organizing a youth ministry to fit your needs.

   Bibliography: p.
   1. Church work with youth—Handbooks, manuals, etc.
I. Potts, Kenneth C. II. Title.
BV4447.J66 1983   259'.2   83-4290
ISBN 0-8170-1004-1

Contents

Approaches to Youth Ministry

Youth ministry is everything that the church does with and for youth
and everything that youth do with and through the church.
That's right. Everything!
That means that when the youth group gets together on Sunday, that's
youth ministry;
when the pastor plays handball with a youth, that's youth ministry;
when youth and adults from the church become involved in the
support of an important social concern, that's youth ministry;
when youth attend morning worship, that's youth ministry;
when the trustees vote to let youth paint and use a room in the
church, that's youth ministry;
when youth and adults from the church spend a day at an amuse-
ment park, that's youth ministry;
when the youth group from the church visits people in a nursing
home, that's youth ministry.

Youth ministry is *everything* the church does with and for youth and
everything youth do with and through the church. This is the central fact
with which we as youth leaders have to come to terms in organizing to
do youth ministry. This concept of youth ministry is both our problem
and our hope. It's our problem because it means that we have the mo-
mentous task of trying to organize *everything*—not just a meeting or a
class or a group—but *everything*. It's also our hope because it means
that the sky's the limit for what we can do in youth ministry. We're not
restricted by a program or a set meeting time or a predetermined structure. We can do anything. We can do *everything!*

Three Types of Activities

Our first task in organizing is to get a handle on this "everything"

that is youth ministry. We'll do that by taking a look at the various pieces
that go together to make youth ministry come alive. These pieces are
the activities that make up the church's ministry with youth—everything
from church school class to the basketball team, from a ski trip to
worship.

To make sense out of all of those pieces, we can put them into three
general categories.

There are *meeting activities,* such as
        church school,
        youth choir,
        Bible study groups,
        prayer breakfasts.
Meeting activities are activities that a group does on a regular basis—
usually weekly or biweekly.

There are *event activities,* such as
        trips,
        retreats,
        fund raisers,
        youth conventions,
        service projects,
        festivals.
Event activities are activities that a group does on a periodic basis—
usually a single event or a series of events held on a monthly or bimonthly basis.

There are *individual activities,* such as
        going out for a snack,
        counseling,
        worship leadership,
        involvement on church boards,
        going to a sports event.
Individual activities are activities that are done on a one-to-one basis.
The frequency with which they occur doesn't matter.

A few more words will help to clarify the differences among these
types of activities. Meeting activities and event activities are both done
with groups; that means that at times distinguishing between them may
be difficult. The major factor is the timing. If an activity is done with

regularity (most often that means weekly or biweekly), it is a meeting activity. If it is done periodically (no more than once a month), then it probably is an event activity. Another factor (although not as important) is the specialness of the activity. Event activities should be seen as special happenings, while meeting activities are part of the ordinary pattern.

Individual activities focus on the development of a one-to-one relationship. They are not concerned with the development of the group. It is possible that an adult might do something with two or three youth and this would still be an individual activity. If the focus is on developing the individual relationship (instead of providing a group experience), it is an individual activity.

With this understanding of types of activities, we can now go a step further and make two statements about how the activities can be put together to form a youth ministry.

Statement 1: Most churches include all three types of activities in their youth ministry.

Statement 2: Most churches can build their most effective youth ministry by centering that ministry on one type of activity.

Here are three examples that illustrate ways in which the three types of activities can fit together.

Example: Most of the youth involved in the youth program at Trinity Church attend the same school. The church has separate junior high and senior high church school classes and a combined youth group. Periodically during the year there are study groups for those youth who want to commit themselves to deeper study of a specific topic. Several times during the year youth work together on fund-raising projects. During the summer, youth participate in a series of recreational activities, such as a canoe trip. The minister and youth group advisors make it a point to attend activities (such as concerts and athletic events) in which church youth participate. Youth frequently drop by the advisors' home for informal talks. Every once in a while, youth are involved in short-term counseling with the minister. *Trinity Church has a Meeting-Centered Approach to youth ministry because the activities that carry the major weight of its youth program (are the center of that program) are meeting activities (church school classes, fellowship groups, and study groups).*

Example: The youth at First Church attend several different schools; so they see one another only at church. The senior high youth group has five weekend retreats during the school year plus a few social events. The junior high group meets for the day on a Saturday once a month. There are separate junior high and senior high church school classes that meet each Sunday morning. Several youth participate on church boards. Two youth spend a day every now and then fishing with an adult in the church who also likes to fish. *First Church has an Event-Centered Approach to youth ministry because the activities that carry the major weight of its youth program (are the center of that program) are event activities (retreats and once-a-month gatherings).*

Example: There are three youth who are related to Calvary Church. One youth is an active member of the board of Christian education. Another has an avid interest in cars; so a church member who is a mechanic makes a point of getting together with her at least once a month to do repair work. The third youth is involved with several adults from the church who visit a nearby retirement home once a month. The pastor frequently involves the youth in worship leadership. Together the youth attend the regional youth events that are sponsored by the denomination. *Calvary Church has an Individual-Centered Approach to youth ministry because the activities that carry the major weight of its youth program (are the center of that program) are relationship activities (one-to-one relationships with adults in the church).*

Which Approach for Your Church?

Which approach will be most effective in a church depends upon several factors.

First, consider the purpose of the church's youth ministry. The approach that is chosen should enable the church's youth ministry's purpose to be accomplished. (See Appendix C.)

Second, look at the youth. The approach that is chosen should enable the church to reach the youth it wants to involve.

Third, be aware of the setting. The approach that is chosen should respond to the larger setting of community, home, work, and school in which the ministry takes place.

Appendix A contains a questionnaire entitled, "Deciding on the Approach for Our Church." If you fill it out and then use the tally sheet to interpret your answers, you'll have a good indication of the approach that may be most effective for your church. If you're working with a group, have the group members discuss each question and decide together how it should be answered.

You may discover that answers are different, depending upon which age group of youth you are considering. If that's true, then complete the questionnaire twice—once for junior highs and once for senior highs. Some churches find that the most effective overall youth ministry is one that uses different approaches for each age level. For example, the junior highs, because of fewer commitments, might function quite well using a Meeting-Centered Approach, while the hectic life-style of senior highs might necessitate an Event-Centered Approach. Or the quirk of the birth pattern in a church might mean that there are three junior high youth and fifteen senior high youth, which could indicate an Individual-Centered Approach for junior highs and a Meeting-Centered or Event-Centered Approach for senior highs. This may not be true for your church, but be open to the possibilities if the answers to the questionnaire seem to indicate the need.

Once you have completed the tally sheet, you will have an indication of the approach that is most appropriate for your church. But since no questionnaire is foolproof, it's important to take a few moments to reflect on what you came up with to see if the conclusion really does make sense. Here are some questions that can help you in that reflection. (If you are working with a group, it would be good to write these questions on newsprint or a chalkboard so that everyone can see them.)

How do you feel about the approach that you came up with?

Does it make sense to you?

Do you believe that it will work in your church?

Will it help you to overcome some difficulties you have had in doing youth ministry?

Will it enable you to achieve the church's purpose for its youth ministry?

If you answer yes to these questions, then you're ready to move on.

If you answer no to any of them, explore the reasons for that answer. Are the reasons strong enough to rule out considering the approach any further? If so, then you might want to consider the approach that came in second on the tally sheet. If not, then go ahead and consider the approach further, but come back to the questions later and see if your concerns have been answered.

You may have decided upon an approach that is different from anything your church has ever done in youth ministry. If so, the prospect of starting something all new may be a bit frightening. That's to be expected. Just remember that what you are trying to do is to develop a youth ministry that fits your unique church. In order to do that you have to believe that you are the experts. You don't need to rely on someone who knows nothing about your church to tell you how to organize and what to do with youth. When it comes to knowing your church and the youth who are in it, you really are the experts!

Now you're ready to move on to developing the particular approach you have selected.

If you chose the Meeting-Centered Approach, turn to chapter 2.

If you chose the Event-Centered Approach, turn to chapter 3.

If you chose the Individual-Centered Approach, turn to chapter 4.

These chapters provide a basic model for each approach. Each chapter has suggestions on the activities to use, a schedule for using the activities, and suggestions about the leadership that is needed. The model suggested will not work forever, though. When it's time to move on to another model, the material in chapter 5 will help you to do that. But first, turn to the chapter that deals with the approach that was your first choice.

Special Note: The Questionnaire (Appendix A) will be most effective if there is common agreement on your church's youth ministry purpose. If you do not have a statement of purpose, the material in Appendix C will be helpful.

A Meeting-Centered Approach | 2

The **Meeting-Centered Approach** is based on regularly scheduled gatherings of youth held on a weekly or biweekly basis. The key is the meeting: a time to share personal concerns and needs, a time to socialize, a time to learn, a time for recreation, a time for mission, a time for evangelism.

Strengths: The Meeting-Centered Approach enables consistent and ongoing group life and friendships. It offers a Christian support group to young people who are struggling and provides the security of a consistent, dependable time each week for the youth to get together. It gives youth a chance to study a topic in depth over a long period of time or tackle a project that might take a number of weeks to complete. The regularity reduces the complexity of planning and the need to publicize meetings.

Weaknesses: The Meeting-Centered Approach makes frequent demands on the time of youth and adults. It may be difficult to find interesting things to do week after week. It can often create a clique of church youth that is difficult for an outsider to break into. It tends primarily to attract youth who are already involved in the church. It depends upon youth being able to get together fairly easily.

If you are just starting a youth program in your church *or* if you are trying this approach for the first time *or* if you are uncertain just what the best way to begin might be, read on!

What is suggested here will not be the way to do things forever. In fact, in a matter of weeks or months you will probably discover that change is needed. That's okay. No structure should be eternal, because people and situations change. But this is a place to begin. When further change seems to be needed, chapter 5 will give you some help.

A basic model for a Meeting-Centered Approach would include:

Church School—Youth can meet for forty-five minutes to one hour on Sunday morning, using church school curriculum materials as the basis for the session.

Youth Group —A regular youth meeting can be held for one and a half hours on Sunday evening (or a weekday evening, if that is more convenient), using youth group program books as the basis for the meeting.

Plus   —Other types of activities can occur on an occasional basis: a fall or spring retreat, a recreational event, a camp or conference, involvement in worship—whatever makes sense to you and the youth.

Depending upon the number of youth involved, any of these activities can be done in separate junior high and senior high groups or in a single group that combines both junior and senior highs. As a general rule, if there would be four or more youth in each church school class, have separate classes for junior highs and senior highs; if there would be eight or more youth in each youth group, have separate groups for junior highs and senior highs.

If there are fewer youth than this, combine the junior highs and senior highs. Combined groups do work! They can provide an exciting and meaningful experience for youth. Although the age span is large, any difficulties that it may present can be made up for by the sense, which the combined group offers, of being together with others. Appendix F provides guidelines for combined groups.

The leadership for this model can be most simply provided by teams.

Adults—Teams of two or three adults each should be formed. If each team could work with a church school class or youth group, that would be ideal but not essential. Most important is to have adults who care about youth and who communicate that caring in relationships with youth. Support for these adults is vital. So if there is only one adult for each class or group, these adults should get together with one another to share thoughts about themselves and about the youth with whom they're working.

Youth —Youth leaders in the groups will enable more effective planning, increase the youth's sense of ownership, and decrease the work load that is placed on the adults. Begin with a minimum number of youth officers—a president and a treasurer (if money is handled by the group). Involve other youth in leadership on an *ad hoc* basis, as needs arise and interests develop.

An Illustration: Grace Church has separate church school classes for junior highs and senior highs with about five youth in each class. The youth group meets regularly on Wednesday evenings. It is for both junior and senior highs. On a typical night about twelve youth are present. Usually the evening begins with a time of fellowship, sometimes including some games. This is followed by a program, which is taken from one of the several resource books the church has purchased. On some nights, instead of the regular program, the group may have an informal discussion or simply do something as a group. About once a month the youth group has a special event. In September and May it is a weekend retreat. At other times it may be a recreational event, involvement in a denominational youth convention or conference, a dinner, or a Christmas party.

An Event-Centered Approach

3

The **Event-Centered Approach** is based on a series of major experiences held on a monthly to bimonthly basis. The key is the event itself: something that is new, different, exciting, and attractive.

Strengths: The Event-Centered Approach does not make frequent demands on the time of youth and adults but, rather, captures their attention and creates enthusiasm with special activities. It allows a chance to tackle ideas or projects intensely for short periods. This approach tends to attract more people, especially youth who are not otherwise involved in the church. It can also provide time blocks of significant length for youth to be together.

Weaknesses: The Event-Centered Approach may mean only infrequent contact with youth, which may lead toward a lack of consistency in attendance. It is difficult to come up with new, different, exciting, and attractive ideas or events on a consistent basis. This style also relies on extensive publicity and advanced planning.

If at the end of chapter 1 you decided on the Event-Centered Approach, take a few minutes now to read this chapter. It suggests a structure based on the Event-Centered Approach. If this structure makes sense to you for your church, then give it a try. If you do not believe the suggested structure will work in your church, then move on to chapter 5 and follow its steps for determining your own structure.

If you do decide to follow the structure suggested in this chapter, do not expect that you will be able to do things this way for an extended period of time. In a matter of months or even weeks you may discover that change is needed. That's okay. No structure should be eternal, because people and situations change. At that point chapter 5 will help you to decide what to do. But for now this can be a place to begin.

A basic model for an Event-Centered Approach would include:

17

Retreats—Several (three to five) retreats spaced over the year will provide extended periods of time for the youth to be together. This will enable meaningful community building and give time to deal with important issues in some depth.

Social Events —Christmas, the end of school, and other significant times can be celebrated with parties, dinners, or other social events.

Trip —A major event that can be worked on over a period of several months would be a camping trip or mission trip during a school vacation.

Joint Events —To provide contact with youth beyond the church, plan for involvement in an area or regional youth convention or spend a weekend with the youth of another church.

Plus —Church school can be held on a regular basis, either as a combined junior high-senior high class or with separate classes for junior highs and senior highs. Personal time with individual youth should be arranged as appropriate.

Any of the event activities can be done with junior highs and senior highs together or in two different groups. The key factor in making the decision should be size. Generally speaking, if fewer than eight youth would be involved in separate group activities, it would be better to plan to do the events on a combined-group basis. Appendix F provides guidelines for combined groups.

This model can function best with team leadership.

Adults—A team of adults can work with youth on a regular basis. It would not be essential for the entire team to be involved in each event, although there should be some continuity in leadership between successive events.

Youth —A planning team of youth can be selected at each major event and given the responsibility of working with the adult leader team to plan the next major event and any activities that take place before that event. There are two ways to provide some continuity from event to event: (1) select one or two persons to serve a full year on the planning team, or (2) rotate the planning team membership so that up to one-half of the members remain as others leave and new members join the planning team.

An Illustration: Youth at First Church participate in two separate groups—one for senior highs, the other for junior highs. The senior high group has five weekend retreats during the school year plus a few social events. They also attend their denomination's regional youth convention each fall. The junior high group meets for the day on a Saturday once a month. Each summer the groups go together on a camping trip or a mission trip. There are separate junior high and senior high church school classes that meet each Sunday morning.

Six adults are on the senior high leader team. At least four of them attend each event. The four who will attend the event also work with the youth in planning it. Two adults work with the junior high group. They are involved in all the junior high events. There is one teacher for each of the two church school classes. Adults in the church who have a special interest in camping are involved in the summer camping trip.

The senior high youth select a president and treasurer to serve for the year; three youth are chosen at each retreat to work with them and the adult leaders in planning the next retreat. The junior highs select two youth at each meeting to work with the adults in planning the next meeting. Planning for the summer trip is done by a group of three junior highs, three senior highs, and two adults.

An Individual-Centered Approach | 4

The **Individual-Centered Approach** is based on one-to-one relationships between youth and adults and youth and youth who interact at home, church, school, and elsewhere. These interactions may involve counseling, learning a skill, recreation, study, or casual conversation, or the interaction might be part of a program leading to baptism and church membership. Youth are also encouraged to be part of the total church family rather than just their own separate youth group. Youth and adults may be assigned to one another, or pairs may be encouraged to form informally from a pool of youth and adults who are interested in this type of ministry with youth. The key is the individual relationship that is developed.

Strengths: The Individual-Centered Approach uses the strengths, interests, and concerns of youth and adults as resources. It encourages the development of strong friendships. It can easily include church and nonchurch youth and is appealing to those who do not like or are not accepted in group-based activities. It does not require large numbers of youth but can work well with even one or two young people. It is based on meeting the needs of each young person as an individual. It also helps youth to see themselves as a part of the total church. This approach does not call for extra space or money from a church.

Weaknesses: The Individual-Centered Approach does not offer youth a chance to develop Christian, peer-group support in learning, relaxing, and serving together. It requires a heavy investment in adult leadership (ideally, one adult for each youth).

This chapter describes one model for the Individual-Centered Approach. It may provide a beginning point for your church, if you have decided on this approach for your youth ministry. If you decide to base the youth ministry on this model, do not expect that you will be able to continue this way indefinitely. In a matter of months or even weeks you may discover that change is needed. That's okay. No one structure should last forever, because people and situations change. When that change takes place, you will need to make adjustments in the approach. At that point, chapter 5 will provide help for you. But for now, this can be a place to begin.

A basic model for an Individual-Centered Approach would include:

Interest   —Pair each youth with an adult who has a similar interest.
Pairings   The interest might be a career, a hobby, a role in the church, or anything else.

Worship   —The pastor can plan for active involvement of youth in
Involvement   worship. This not only should include youth doing traditional parts of the service but also encourage fuller involvement by having youth share their own worship expressions.

Informal   —The pastor and other church members should be inten-
Visits   tional about getting together with youth on an informal but regular basis. This can be for pizza and a soda after school. It is a time to check in and demonstrate a continuing interest in the youth as persons.

Plus   —Even with just a few youth in the church, it is possible to have a church school class. Involvement in interchurch activities sponsored by the denomination can also be part of an individual-centered approach. These might be conventions, conferences, or rallies—any activity in which the youth can be together with peers and sense being part of a large community.

This approach needs no formal leadership. All that is required is the involvement of a number of adults who are willing and able to develop meaningful relationships with youth.

An Illustration: At Immanuel Church several youth-adult pairs get together periodically to pursue common interests: one pair regularly attends athletic events; another gets together to play guitars; another to do weaving and other handwork; while still another works to bring concerns of peace and justice before the church. One youth, who has a special interest in young children, is part of the teaching team for the primary class. The pastor asks youth to participate in worship leadership on a regular basis.

The church encourages participation of its youth in denomination-sponsored youth events. These include the regional youth conventions and national youth conferences. Money is available from the church budget for youth who wish to participate in these events.

Developing Your Own Approach

5

If you began with any of the models suggested in the preceding chapters, you will reach a point when you and/or the youth conclude that the model you are using doesn't really meet the youth's needs. This may become apparent right away or it may take some time, but it will happen. We can be certain of that because any structure must help the people who use it to have their needs met in the situation in which they find themselves. People (especially youth) and situations change; so youth ministry structures, to be effective, must constantly evolve. Don't see the need to change the ministry as failure; it's only a sign of growth!

Some of the indications that changes in structure may be needed are:
— conflicts between youth ministry activities and other involvements youth have;
— a loss of energy and creativity on the part of the adults and/or the youth;
— "suspicious" excuses by youth about why they can't make it to meetings;
— the inability to involve adults as leaders;
— a lack of continuing personal growth and development within the group;
— declining attendance;
— a self-satisfaction and contentedness on the part of the group;
— more and more work being done by fewer and fewer people;
— youth attending only the "fun" events;
— youth saying, "We'd like to, but. . . ."

If any of these symptoms become evident in your church's youth ministry, then it may be time to look again at the way in which the youth program is structured. We tend to look at leaders, youth, or resources as the cause of problems in the youth program. While these may be factors, the structure of the program is very likely a major reason for problems. Following the suggestions that are offered here will help you to confront and deal with the issue of structure.

Before we begin, however, a few words of caution: No process for making decisions about structure is foolproof. We will try to look at some important issues and ask some important questions, but ultimately what is decided needs to rely on your own sense of what will work, your own willingness to risk, and your own ability to look creatively at your situation. That probably sounds scary. It is in a sense. But it is also possible—quite possible. It will be easier for you to handle if

—you involve others (both youth and adults) with you;

—you believe the problems are solvable;

—you trust your sense of what "seems right";

—you remember that your creativity really is God's Spirit at work through you.

Now, let's get to work!

1. Use the "Deciding on the Approach for Our Church" Worksheets

To begin the process, review the material in chapter 1 and complete the worksheets in Appendix A again. You may have used the worksheets in choosing the present structure, but enough factors may have changed since that time to indicate that a different approach is needed now.

You may complete the worksheet on your own. However, the results are likely to be more meaningful if a group of people is brought together to do the work of structuring the youth program. If you are working with a group, decide together how each question should be answered, discussing any answer about which the group members may have a difference of opinion until the group reaches a consensus. If consensus is impossible, answer according to the majority opinion. Make every effort to reach consensus first.

When you have completed the tally sheet and made your decision about the basic approach, do a reality check by answering the following questions.

Does the approach that you came up with feel right for you?

Does it make sense to you?

Do you believe that it will work in your church?

Will it help you to overcome the difficulties you have had in doing youth ministry?

Will it enable you to achieve the church's purpose for its youth ministry?

If you can answer yes to these questions, then you're ready to move on to the next step.

If you answer no to any of them, explore the reasons for that answer. Are the reasons strong enough to rule out considering the approach any further? If so, then you might want to consider the approach that came in second on the tally sheet. If you still feel that the first approach is best, then move on to step 2, but come back to the questions later and see if your concerns have been answered.

2. Make Two Decisions About Who Will Be Involved

(For those who selected either the Meeting-Centered Approach or the Event-Centered Approach.)

These two decisions may in fact be assumptions you have had all along or givens that you can do nothing about. Or it may be that the options suggested have never been considered as real possibilities. Regardless of how these questions have been dealt with in the past, it will be good to consider them now.

   a) Will you do the youth program independently as a church or jointly with another church?

   b) Will the youth group be a combined junior high-senior high group, or will you have separate groups for junior highs and senior highs?

The most obvious factor to consider in answering these questions is size. A youth program that is done jointly with another church or that combines junior high and senior high youth may provide the numbers for a significant group that would not be possible in independent or separate junior high and senior high programs. A joint or combined program may also be a more effective way to use a limited number of leaders because there will be fewer events or meetings than there would be with two separate groups.

There are also disadvantages to joint and combined programs that should be considered. A program done jointly with another church usually reduces the opportunities for involving youth in the total life of the church; the youth program can more easily become isolated from the life of either church. A combined junior high-senior high program will mean a wide age span of youth; this can make difficult the planning of a program that appeals to all and may result in the growing uninvolvement of youth at either end of the age span. (See Appendix F for further information about combined junior high-senior high groups.)

The decision you make will depend upon your own particular situation. What is important is that you make the decision consciously after considering both the advantages and disadvantages.

Note: If you have selected a joint or combined program in order to have enough youth for a group but are not really comfortable with your decision, consider again the possibility of an Individual-Centered Approach. This is a nongroup approach and so the number of youth does not matter.

---

3. Decide on Core Activities

Core activities are those activities in which you spend the most time and accomplish most of your purpose. They are the activities on which the youth program will be based—the foundation for everything else that is done. Therefore, if in step 1 you decided on a Meeting-Centered Approach, the core activities should be meeting activities; if you decided on an Event-Centered Approach, the core activities should be event activities; if you decided on an Individual-Centered Approach, the core activities should be individual activities. Appendix B contains a list of possible youth ministry activities arranged according to three types of activities. To decide on the core activities for your church's youth program, do the following:

a) Read over the list of activities related to the approach you selected in step 1. Add any other activities of the same type that you can think of. Build as long a list as possible. Don't worry about being realistic at this point; just be certain that the activities meet the criteria for the approach that you selected: meeting activities are done by a group on a weekly or biweekly basis; event activities are done by a group on a periodic basis; individual activities are done on a person-to-person basis. (If you are working with a group, put the list of activities on newsprint or a chalkboard so that everyone can see it and then add additional activities to the list.)

b) Check any activities that you believe might be workable and effective in your church. (If you are working with a group, check the activities on the newsprint or chalkboard.)

c) Evaluate each of the checked activities by asking:

What are the values (advantages) of this activity?

What might be some problems (disadvantages) related to this activity?

How would we do this in our church?

(If you are working with a group, have the entire group discuss these questions for each checked activity. Ask one person to record the major points related to each activity on newsprint.)

d) On the basis of your answers to the questions, select one or two activities that will be the core of the youth program. (If you are working with a group, have the group reach consensus on the activity or activities that you use.)

e) After you have made a selection, describe the activity or activities by using the following outline.

What is the activity?

Who will be included?

When will it happen?

(If you are working with a group, put this on newsprint so that everyone can see it.)

f) Before you move on, look again at the activity or activities you have chosen. Does the selection make sense to you as the basis for your church's youth program? Are you comfortable with it? If yes, move on to the next step. If no, explore the reason for your discomfort and make any changes that will help. (If you are working with a group, have the group as a whole discuss these questions.)

4. Decide on Supplemental Activities

It is the rare youth program that can thrive (or even survive) on a steady diet of one type of activity. The diet needs to be supplemented with activities from the other two types. What follows will help you decide which supplemental activities will work best in your church's youth program.

a) Read the lists (from Appendix B) of the two types of activities not considered in step 3 and add whatever additional activities you can think of. (In a group, put the lists on newsprint and add additional activities to the newsprint.)

b) Check all those activities that you (or a member of the group) believe would be workable and effective if put into use in your church.

c) Evaluate the checked activities by asking:

Which activities will help overcome problems (disadvantages) of the core activity or activities that you selected?

Which activities does the church have the resources to do? Which activities do people (youth and adults) have the time to do?

Which activities will do most to make the church's youth ministry exciting, attractive, and responsive to the needs of youth, what concerned adults and youth really want it to be?

d) On the basis of your answers to these questions, select additional activities to supplement the core activities you chose in step 3. The number of activities you choose will depend upon the number of times you plan to do each one, the leadership that is available, and the total amount of time you want to involve in the supplemental activities.

5. Write a Description of the Youth Program

As a way of organizing the work you've done, write a description of the youth program that the church will be offering for the next several months. Include in the description the following:

—the purpose (Appendix C),

—the activities that will be offered (both core and supplemental),

—the youth that will be involved, and

—the times that the activities will take place.

When the description is written, take time for another reality check. Does the total program make sense to you? Is it workable? Will it allow you to accomplish what you have determined that you want to accomplish in youth ministry?

6. Decide on the Leadership That Is Needed

Now that you have a picture of the youth program, you can decide on the leadership—that is, the adults and youth who will enable the program to work.

Adult Leaders

Think *team!* That's the key for recruiting, keeping, and enabling the effectiveness of adults who work with youth. Teams of two, three, or more adults can work in each of the major program areas (for example, church school, youth group meetings, trips). The advantages of a team are that a team provides the following:

—a variety of models and kinds of adults for youth to relate to;
—support for team members;
—sharing of responsibilities, which means less time and effort for all;
—a continuity of leadership without the same person having to do everything.

The adult leadership team should meet periodically for planning and support, especially focusing on the development of relationships with all the youth who participate in the program.

The key roles of the adults on the leader team are the following:

—to model; to demonstrate by their behavior the meaning of the Christian faith as it relates to daily living.
—to enable; to guide youth in becoming the persons God intends them to be; to help them in discovering their gifts; to challenge them to use their gifts; to support them as they try, sometimes failing, sometimes succeeding.
—to promote group development (when working with a group); to encourage Christian community among the youth as they seek to understand the meaning of being a Christian group and what that meaning implies for their behavior toward one another and those outside the group.
—to advise and support; to act as a listener/counselor for youth, being aware of the need to refer serious problems to professionally trained counselors.
—to mediate; to assist in problems that arise among youth and, when asked, between parents, teachers, others, and youth.
—to act as an intermediary: to act as an advocate of the youth and/or the youth group within the church family and the community.

—to supervise; to make youth aware of times when their behavior is inappropriate in a particular situation; to protect other persons and property; to bring minor disciplinary problems to the attention of the group; to bring major disciplinary problems to the attention of those persons who should be involved in their resolution.

The illustrations in chapters 2 through 4 provide specific examples of ways in which adult leader teams can function. They can be a beginning point for you. What will work best for you depends upon how you apply the principle of the adult leader team to the program structure you have decided upon together with the persons in your church who are able and willing to work with youth.

Youth Leaders

There are two basic styles for the youth leadership: the cabinet style and the task-force style.

The *Cabinet Style* is based on elected officers. These officers are often a president, a vice president, a secretary, and a treasurer. But it is important that all officers have specific duties and sufficient work to involve them meaningfully in the work of the cabinet. In most cases all of the officers would be chosen by the entire group. However, in very large groups it is also possible to select representatives from the age groups or classes. All officers serve a fixed term, usually a year. The strength of the cabinet style is that it provides an ongoing group of persons with specific responsibilities for the youth program. Its major weaknesses are that it has little flexibility and that it can lead to the establishment of a leadership elite in the group.

The *Task-Force Style* is based on a group of youth who are selected in order to perform a specific task (for example, plan a retreat). It may be of any size, although a group any larger than six or seven may become difficult to work with. There may be several task forces that exist at one time, each working on a different task. The advantages of the task-force style are its flexibility and the involvement of a large number of youth in leadership. Its major disadvantages are the need for coordination among the task forces it presents and the lack of continuity that can result from having no persons who carry the same responsibilities over a period of time.

While these are the two basic styles, it is also possible to create a new style by combining these two in a variety of ways. Your church may discover that a *Combination Style* works most effectively with your youth program. One form that the combination style might take is the selection of one or two youth to serve for an entire year. If appropriate, specific titles, such as president and treasurer, may be given to these persons. Other youth can then be selected for leadership on a short-term basis related to a specific task or tasks. This combination style still provides for the involvement of a large number of youth in leadership but also allows for continuity through the continuing involvement of the youth who have been selected to serve on a long-term basis.

In deciding what style of youth leadership is most appropriate for your youth program, it is most important to keep in mind those two concerns: (1) the responsibilities that need to be filled, and (2) the means of most effectively involving participants in the planning and doing. Look over the youth program description you have written in light of these two concerns. When you have done this, it should be possible to determine which of the styles described will be most appropriate.

The illustrations in chapters 2 through 4 provide specific examples of youth leadership for a variety of youth programs. They may be an additional help for you in making your decision.

Conclusion 6

The work that this book describes is one part of building an effective youth ministry in your church. The plan suggested here doesn't guarantee success. Following the plan won't mean that you will suddenly find yourself with more youth than you know what to do with or that problems and criticism will disappear.

What is suggested here is a very important element in developing a youth program. It provides the foundation—we hope the right foundation—upon which you can build. It permits effective building; it doesn't guarantee it. Your concern now is to do that effective building—most importantly that you do that effective building in the quality of relationships that you and others in the youth program develop. In a real sense, what we've done here is to create the context in which those relationships have a good chance to develop. These relationships need to be enabled by every part of the youth program: the Bible study, the recreation, the official functions, the fun times together, the mission you are involved in.

The key to all of this is openness—the openness of you and youth to one another and to the Spirit of God at work in your midst. This openness often results in change, both in persons and in structures. As has been said frequently in this book, that's okay. Change is too often seen as a sign of failure. It shouldn't be. Rather, change is a sign of growth, a sign of responding to new needs and situations, a sign of openness to the Spirit.

As you work through this book and as you continue the building, keep that in mind. Most importantly, remember that you and others in your church's ministry with youth are called to the important, challenging, and fulfilling mission of doing God's work with youth. And the God who calls also enables.

Appendix A

Questionnaire: Deciding on the Approach for Our Church

Part I. Check the answers that best describe our church:

Which youth does the church want to involve in its youth program?

1. ____ Youth whose families belong to the church.

9. ____ Youth both within and outside the church.

How would you describe the youth that the church wants to involve?

2. ____ Relatively free of nonchurch involvements.

10. ____ Heavily involved in nonchurch activities.

How well do the youth know one another?

3. ____ Quite well.

11. ____ Not very well.

How comfortable are the youth with one another?

4. ____ Quite comfortable.

12. ____ Not very comfortable.

What school(s) do youth attend?

5. ____ Most attend the same school.

13. ____ Most attend different schools.

How far do most youth live from the church?

6. ____ Within easy walking or driving distance.

14. ____ Beyond easy walking or driving distance.

What are the feelings of the youth about getting together?

7. ____ They like to get together regularly.

15. ____ Although they like getting together, they won't or can't do it often.

17. ____ They do not enjoy being together.

What is the adult feeling about involvement in the youth program?

8. ____ There are adults who are willing and able to meet with youth regularly.

16. ____ There are adults who are willing to work with a group, but they are unable to spend the time to meet regularly.

18. ____ A number of adults are willing and able to relate with youth but do not want to conduct a youth program.

Part II. Check all those statements that you believe describe our church.

____ 1. Youth are committed to learning about and experiencing their faith on a regular basis.

____ 2. The youth spend time together throughout the week.

____ 3. The church building has space that can be set aside permanently for a youth meeting/lounge/recreation area.

____ 4. The church is a gathering place for youth.

____ 5. The youth want to try a variety of different things as part of the youth program.

____ 6. There is money available from the youth themselves and within the church for special events.

____ 7. There are a number of facilities and resources for different kinds of activities in the area.

____ 8. Youth and adults are willing to spend time in advance planning and publicity.

____ 9. We want to place an emphasis on responding to the unique needs of individual youth rather than responding to needs youth have in common.

____ 10. One of our primary concerns is to make youth an integral part of all church activities (committees, boards, worship, church school).

____ 11. The church has few resources it can devote to a youth program.

___ 12. There are not enough youth in the church for a significant group.

Tally Sheet: Interpreting the Responses

	A	B	C

In Part I, how many checks did you have in each of the following groupings? Record your answers on the lines provided.

Answers 1-8 _____ (A)

Answers 9-16 _____ (B)

Answers 9-14, 17, 18 _____ (C)

In Part II, how many checks did you have in each of the following groupings? Record your answers on the lines provided.

Statements 1-4 _____ (A)

Statements 5-8 _____ (B)

Statements 9-12 _____ (C)

What is the total of each column?   A___ B___ C___

The column that has the greatest number of checks indicates the approach that is likely to be most appropriate for your church.

Column with Most Checks	Most Appropriate Approach
A	Meeting-Centered Approach
B	Event-Centered Approach
C	Individual-Centered Approach

Appendix B

Youth Ministry Activities

Meeting Activities

church school
Bible study group
sport team
sharing group
drama group
outreach group
fellowship group
youth choir
prayer breakfast
recreation nights
study groups
newspaper

Event Activities

retreats
vacation church school
service projects
social events
seminars
hikes
athletic events
seasonal celebrations
recognition programs
prayer vigils
trips
cluster/state/region/city denominational events
festivals
fund raisers
camping
exchanges with other churches
performances

Individual Activities

going out for a snack
relationships with church officers
counseling
attending school events
worship involvement
attending special events
teaching special skills
visiting shut-ins
dropping by homes
involvement on church board
running a coffee house
teaming with adults who have similar skill or career interests
birthday activities

Appendix C

Deciding on a Statement of Purpose

There are two parts to ministry with youth: ministry to youth and ministry by youth. A youth ministry purpose statement should deal with both kinds of ministry. It deals with ministry to youth by answering the question "What will happen to the youth?" It deals with ministry by youth by answering the question "What will the youth do?"

Possible answers to "What will happen to the youth?" are that youth will:

____ grow in faith;

____ develop a positive self-concept;

____ see their faith as central to their identity;

____ increase their knowledge of the Bible;

____ see the relationship of faith to important issues in their lives;

____ grow in their ability to develop honest, open, caring relationships;

____ be part of a caring Christian community;

____ grow in understanding their role in the church's ministry;

____ develop a better understanding of themselves as females or males;

____ grow in their relationships with parents and other significant adults;

____ develop meaningful values that can be used to make life-style decisions;

____ be prepared for the future;

____ develop better relationships with their brothers and sisters.

Possible answers to "What will the youth do?" are that youth will:

____ participate in the life of the church;

____ share in worship leadership;

_____ become involved in mission;

_____ live as Christians at school;

_____ respond, as individuals and/or a group, to significant social issues;

_____ become involved in evangelism;

_____ live as Christians in their families.

The following process may be helpful to you in determining a statement of purpose for your church's youth ministry.

1. Review the preceding lists, checking any items that you believe are important for your church.

2. Add any items that you believe are important and are not included on the lists.

3. Select no more than five of the checked items (the ones that you believe are most important and most basic) to be included in the purpose statement.

4. Use these items as the basis for a statement beginning: "The purpose of our ministry with youth is to enable youth to. . . ."

This process will work best if a group, composed of youth and adults, works together to develop the statement. Once the statement is written, it can be shared with other youth and adults in the church for their reactions. These reactions should then be considered by the group, and any changes that are appropriate should be made in the statement.

Appendix D

Foundational Thoughts About Organizing for Ministry with Youth

What does it mean to organize for ministry with youth? Let's begin with some simple defining of terms.

Organize—"to form into a whole, consisting of interdependent or coordinated parts, to systematize." Organization *is* a system. It is a way of taking several pieces that need to be together and fitting them together. Organization usually has a purpose, although it is not unheard of to organize when there is no good reason to do so.

For—"with the intent or purpose of." That's good enough as it is.

Ministry—"the act of giving service, care, or aid." Notice that religious terms, such as clergy and churches, don't appear in the definition. That is not the definition of ministry that we are looking for. We *are* talking about Christian ministry, and that is ministry that is done by *both* volunteers and professionals. Also notice that ministry is not automatically tied to such standard things as youth groups, retreats, or counseling. Those are some possible ways of ministering, but it's important to leave the options open for new areas of ministry. We'll stick with the general terms—service, care, and aid.

With—"in some particular relation to, implying interaction, company, association, conjunction, or connection." This is a more important word than you might at first think. We are not talking about "to" or "for." Those words leave the impression that our ministry is one-sided, a prepackaged something or other that is imposed upon youth by persons (usually adults) who "know more." "With," as our definition tries to say, implies something that is done together—a partnership.

Youth—"young persons, collectively." That seems a little vague. Who (or what) are young persons? What ages does the word "youth" encompass? Basically you'll have to figure that out for yourself. It depends on what you decide best fits your situation. Are twenty-year-olds youths? They might be for you. How about someone who is twelve years old? Again, what makes sense to you and your situation? Generally the lines of definition are drawn close to the teen years, but it's important to be flexible.

Now to pull it all together. What we're concerned about in organizing for ministry with youth is putting together the various pieces of a church's program with young people so that service, care, and aid can be given to them and by them (that is, *with* them) in a Christian context.

But we're not concerned about just *any* kind of organization for ministry with youth. We need to concentrate on *good* organization, not just an organization that does the job, but one that does the job well. There are five basic characteristics of a good organization for ministry with youth. Let's take them one at a time.

First, a good organization for ministry with youth is *simple,* the simpler the better. We have all been involved in situations in which the organizational structure is so complex that we spend most of our time filling out myriads of reports or going through dozens of "proper" channels or whatever. That type of unnecessarily complex organization gets downright trying; eventually it begins to alienate the very people it is supposed to serve. Mark Twain told the story of a steamboat whistle which took so much steam to blow that the boat itself had to stop and build up pressure again before it could make headway. Organizations can be like that whistle. When they are, it's because they're no longer simple.

Second, a good organization for ministry with youth is *adaptable.* Another way of saying this is to say that good organization bends rather than breaks. It adapts to meet new conditions rather than falling apart at the first hint of change or being so rigid that it doesn't permit change.

Of course, in order to adapt effectively we need to know when to adapt. That means keeping our finger on the pulse of the organization. We want to be able to pick up those little (or big) hints that it is time to make some changes in the way we do things. For that reason it's important to be always reevaluating and adapting. Such evaluation and adaptation needs to be built right into an organizational structure. It needs to be planned. One of the last steps in our process of organizing for ministry with youth should be to plan for reevaluation and adaptation!

Third, a good organization for ministry with youth is *inclusive.* That means that it includes people, lots of people, as many people as practical.

(A word about what is meant by "practical": if you are planning a party, for example, you might want only five people involved in the planning; any more people would get confusing. When you hold the party, though, you might want to have fifty people because, in that particular case, the more the merrier.) Being inclusive means involving as many people as it is practical to involve in planning. Being inclusive means involving as many people as it is practical to involve in doing. Being inclusive means involving as many people as it is practical to involve in evaluating and adapting.

Fourth, good organization for ministry with youth is *person centered*. Simply put, that means that good organization recognizes that each person is unique, with different wants and needs, likes and dislikes. Good organization not only recognizes this but also allows for it and actually promotes it. It tries to encourage each person to be all that God made him or her to be, rather than forcing the individual to fit into one particular mold of what someone else believes is proper. Good organization doesn't let procedures, structure, or anything else come before people.

Fifth, a good organization for ministry with youth is *compatible with existing organization*. Ministry with youth is not done in a vacuum. It is part of the total ministry of the church. So it needs to be tied clearly into the church organization. Think in terms of who is responsible for what, who is accountable to whom, and what communication channels need to be set up.

Those are five practical characteristics of good organization for ministry with youth.

It's also important to look at the question of why we should organize. We can start with our call to minister. Simply put, God calls on us to minister with those around us. That includes ministry with youth. The Bible gives us some insights into the way others have responded to their calls through organizing. True, Jesus did not spend a lot of time organizing his disciples. But both Old and New Testaments give some very clear examples in which a good organizational structure was valued.

What was one of the first things that the Hebrews did upon escaping from Egypt? They organized. Priests, Levites, soldiers—all were assigned certain roles, jobs, or responsibilities.

What was one of the first things that the early church did? It organized.

The apostles chose a new apostle to take Judas' place; the church members selected elders, deacons, teachers, and preachers.

The Bible reveals a concern with organization. The parable of the three servants, or the talents, provides some insight into the reason for that concern.

"For it will be as when a man going on a journey called his servants and entrusted to them his property; to one he gave five talents, to another two, to another one, to each according to his ability. Then he went away. He who had received the five talents went at once and traded with them; and he made five talents more. So also, he who had the two talents made two talents more. But he who had received the one talent went and dug in the ground and hid his master's money. Now after a long time the master of those servants came and settled accounts with them. And he who had received the five talents came forward, bringing five talents more, saying, 'Master, you delivered to me five talents; here I have made five talents more.' His master said to him, 'Well done, good and faithful servant; you have been faithful over a little, I will set you over much; enter into the joy of your master.' And he also who had the two talents came forward, saying, 'Master, you delivered to me two talents; here I have made two talents more.' His master said to him, 'Well done, good and faithful servant; you have been faithful over a little, I will set you over much; enter into the joy of your master.' He also who had received the one talent came forward, saying, 'Master, I knew you to be a hard man, reaping where you did not sow, and gathering where you did not winnow; so I was afraid, and I went and hid your talent in the ground. Here you have what is yours.' But his master answered him, 'You wicked and slothful servant! You knew that I reap where I have not sowed, and gather where I have not winnowed? Then you ought to have invested my money with the bankers, and at my coming I should have received what was my own with interest. So take the talent from him, and give it to him who has the ten talents. For to every one who has will more be given, and he will have abundance; but from him who has not, even what he has will be taken away. And cast the worthless servant into the outer darkness; there men will weep and gnash their teeth.' "

—Matthew 25:14-30

One point of Jesus' story is that God calls upon each of us to be good stewards of our resources, which, when we think about it, God has supplied to us. These resources are not just money but include time, effort, materials, and so on. There is a lot to do in God's world; God does not want us wasting our limited resources while we do it. Good organization is theologically sound because its goal is to help us to get the most accomplished by our efforts, to be good stewards of God's gifts. That's important.

So from a theological perspective we are called to minister with persons, and called to be good stewards as we do so. These are good reasons for a Christian to spend some time developing good organization.

Time spent in organizing for ministry with youth is time that is well spent.

Appendix E

Factors Involved in Determining Youth Ministry Organization

Organizing for youth ministry in the church involves two steps. First the structure must be determined, and then the leadership must be provided. Structure is the way a church puts selected youth program activities together to form its ministry with youth. Once the structure has been decided upon, the leadership positions that will enable the structure to function effectively need to be determined. In this section we will look at the important factors that need to be considered in determining the structure and leadership for youth ministry in the local church.

Structure

Structure enables program.

Structure also blocks program and sometimes even makes it impossible.

The frustration and failure that frequently plague churches in their youth ministry, and for which leaders and program resources are often blamed, may have nothing at all to do with people or content. They may arise because a church is attempting to do something that cannot be done, something that its youth ministry structure will not allow to happen. If the conscious purpose of a church's youth ministry is to build Christian community in the youth group but the group meets for only an hour once a week, there will be frustration. If a church wants to extend its youth ministry to the high school but provides programs only in the church building, there will be failure. If a church plans frequent meetings of the youth groups but most families live a distance from the church, there will be frustration and failure.

The best planned and executed program loses much of its potential effectiveness if that program does not happen in a structure that takes into account who the program is attempting to reach, what it is attempting to accomplish, and where it is taking place.

This is why it is essential that every church think carefully about the structure of its youth ministry. In doing that thinking, the church needs to answer three basic questions.

Who do we want to reach through our ministry?
What do we want to accomplish in our ministry?
Where is our ministry taking place?

The answers to these questions will provide a church with information about the three factors that determine effective structure for youth ministry: audience, purpose, and setting.

1. Audience

The first question of concern to a church, as it structures for youth ministry, needs to be "Who do we want to reach through our ministry?" David Evans, in *Shaping the Church's Ministry with Youth,* indicates that there are at least four kinds of youth with whom the church's youth ministry might potentially be concerned.

> *First, there is the young person to whom the Christian faith has meaning and for whom the gathered church experience is significant. . . .*
> *Second, there is the church dropout. . . .*
> *Third, there is the young person for whom our ministry seems to be a kind of "holding process." . . .*
> *Fourth, there is the young person we do not even know, or if we do know him [her], our relationship with him [her] is outside the church fellowship.*[1]

Most often a church's youth ministry involves the first and third kinds of youth. These are the youth who are in the church and for whom the need to do *something* is obvious.

Youth of the second and fourth kinds, however, have no ongoing relationships with the church. Their presence and their needs are not obvious. And most often they are forgotten. They become involved in a church's youth ministry only by chance.

Much of the reason for this is that the structure of youth ministry in most churches does not encourage youth's involvement because the ministry never reaches beyond the church to touch and to involve them

[1]David Evans, *Shaping the Church's Ministry with Youth* (Valley Forge: Judson Press, 1965), pp. 45-48.

where they are. This is not to say that a church's youth ministry *must* be structured in such a way as to reach the "dropout" or the person outside the church. It does say, however, that if reaching them is a concern, then the structure must be one that enables their involvement in a significant way. If a church does not structure youth ministry in this way, it should not expect a significant ministry to the dropout or outsider.

Even in ministry to the involved or "holding" young person, careful thought must be given to who these youth are, what interests they have, and where it is they live their lives. While it may be true that they are in a church building several hours a week, a youth ministry that significantly touches their lives may need to be structured in such a way as to reach them in other times and at other places.

In order to structure its youth ministry effectively, a church must know with whom it wants to minister and how they can be reached.

2. Purpose

The purpose of a church's youth ministry should be to respond to the needs of the youth with whom it wishes to minister. The purpose is founded on those needs and responds to them in light of the gospel.

If there is no commonly stated and understood statement of purpose for a church's youth ministry, members are apt to have differing unconscious and/or unspoken assumptions about the purpose which surface in conflicts over whether or not the church's youth ministry is "successful." More importantly, without this understanding of purpose a church has no basis upon which to plan its youth ministry.

In order to structure its youth ministry effectively, a church needs to have a clear understanding of what it wants to accomplish. (See Appendix C for help in developing a statement of purpose.)

3. Setting

The setting in which the church's youth ministry takes place is the third significant factor that a church needs to consider in structuring its youth ministry. Everything that happens in a church, the family, and the community influences youth ministry. In deciding how to organize, a church needs to look at the most significant influences in order to determine how to take advantage of or work around them.

Influences that are important include other activities in which youth are involved, schools they attend, location of the church, finances, the attitudes of the church, and the youth group itself. If large numbers of youth are actively involved in football and marching band, this influences the type of youth ministry structure that can work effectively in the fall. If most members do not live near the church, this influences the number of church meetings that can be part of the structure. If youth do not see one another at school during the week, this influences the number of "group building" events that should be part of the structure.

In order to structure effectively for youth ministry, a church must understand where its ministry is taking place.

When a church has a good understanding of the three factors of audience, purpose, and setting, it has the knowledge it needs to assess potential activities for its youth ministry. As these individual activities are fitted together, the church's total youth ministry structure is formed. After (a) determining the youth with whom its ministry is to take place, (b) deciding on the purpose of its ministry, and (c) assessing the significant influences that the setting has on its ministry, a church can develop its structure for youth ministry by taking the following additional steps:

d) brainstorming activities that might be part of its ministry;

e) assessing these activities in light of the discoveries made in steps (a), (b), and (c);

f) selecting the activities that most effectively respond to the audience, purpose, and setting;

g) fitting these activities into a total youth ministry structure, keeping in mind that the structure it creates needs to provide simplicity, flexibility, involvement, respect for persons, and compatability with the church organization.

Leadership

In determining the leadership positions that are needed to support its youth ministry structure, a church needs to keep three factors in mind:

—the responsibilities that need to be filled;

—the means of most effectively involving participants in the planning and doing; and

—the appropriate role of adults.

1. Responsibilities

Placing persons, youth or adult, in leadership positions that have no actual duties or responsibilities leads to frustration. Having duties that need to be performed but not having a person in a position with responsibility for them leads to chaos.

So the first question that should be asked in determining what leadership positions a youth ministry structure needs is "What jobs need to be done?" If there are no letters to write or minutes to keep, there's no need for a secretary. But if the group takes a lot of trips, someone needs to be in charge of transportation. Once the jobs that need to be done are determined, they can be grouped together so that those jobs given to a leadership position will be similar and manageable. Then persons (either youth or adult) can be selected to fill the positions. This approach to determining leadership positions should ensure that the jobs that need to be done are done and that every person chosen for leadership does have significant responsibilities.

2. Youth Involvement

One of the keys to an alive youth ministry is youth participation in deciding what ministry is about and what they, as part of that ministry, will do. Therefore, in determining the leadership, a church will want to develop a way to involve as many youth as possible in the planning and decision-making processes. This does not mean that every youth needs to be involved in every decision, but it does say that enough need to be involved so that the decision will reflect the thinking of the group as a whole. And it does say that each youth should be involved in enough decisions to give him or her a sense of ownership of the church's youth ministry. So leadership positions within a church's youth ministry structure need to be determined with careful attention to the question "How can youth be most effectively involved in the planning and doing?"

3. Adult Role

Youth ministry is an intergenerational ministry. It should not be something done "for the kids." Neither should it be something done "by the kids." Youth ministry belongs to both youth and adults who are willing to commit themselves to it. As youth should be involved in the planning and doing, so should adults. The ways in which they are involved will vary depending upon the circumstances, but they should be involved. At all times this adult involvement should be enabling, encouraging, and modeling. So leadership positions within a church's youth ministry structure need to be determined with careful attention to the question "What are the responsibilities that are appropriate to the youth and adults who are committed to our youth ministry?"

Appendix F

Guidelines for Combined Junior High-Senior High Groups

The combined group is a reality for youth ministry in many churches. One-third of all the youth groups in one denomination are combined groups. To be sure there are difficulties when a church develops its youth program this way, but there is also a lot of potential. The purpose of these guidelines is to help your church realize more of its potential.

Each church is different, and its style and approach must allow for uniqueness. But there are some basic principles for successful youth ministry in combined groups. It's not the same as relating to junior highs and senior highs separately. If you are aware of the differences and allow for them as you plan the structure and program of your church's youth ministry, you may be surprised by the results.

Here are the guidelines.

1. The programs must allow for a good bit of activity and should lend themselves to several levels of interpretation and learning. For example, a simulation game will work a lot better than a discussion based on a book; a project has a better chance of success than a speaker.

2. Don't be afraid to do a number of things that are "just for fun." This provides opportunity for the informal interaction that is essential in building relationships. Because most junior highs and senior highs do not automatically gravitate toward one another, the program needs to provide the opportunity for interaction.

3. The structure should allow for youth of the same age group to be together at some times. This might be during church school, as a portion of the regular meeting time, or at other times during the year. Youth of different ages do have concerns that are unique, and it is important to deal with them. These separate get-togethers will provide the opportunity to do this.

4. The structure and program should allow for participation in small groups. At times, as few as four or five youth in a group would be good. This will allow for the building of closer relationships by careful listening and create less anxiety about speaking up. Such small-group participation is important in all types of youth ministry but especially so in combined groups in which younger youth might feel overwhelmed or intimidated.

5. If possible, youth should be given the opportunity to choose how they will be involved. If there is choice, they will have a greater sense of ownership, and age difference will become less significant. Also, offering choices to the youth will have the effect of grouping those with common interests together, further reducing the signifi-cance of age. The opportunity for choices can come through offering electives for study or by involving the group as a whole in the major decisions about what will be done.

6. Keep the needs of the individual foremost. This is a basic for all youth ministry and is vitally important here, too. The structure and program must be flexible enough—you must be flexible enough—to relate to the needs and concerns of all the youth who are involved.

Key Youth Ministry Resources

The letter following each listing indicates in which of the approaches the resource will be most helpful. Most books will be usable in all approaches.

M—Meeting-Centered Approach
E —Event-Centered Approach
I —Individual-Centered Approach

Bible Journeys, Dick Orr and David L. Bartlett. (Valley Forge: Judson Press, 1980) $4.95. A unique resource to help youth in their personal search for Christian growth. Through imaginative, first-person narrative, the Bible comes alive. (M, E)

Building an Effective Youth Ministry, Glenn E. Ludwig. (Nashville: Abingdon Press, 1979) $4.95. General resource book dealing with issues such as structure, programming, adult role, and administration. (M)

The Care and Counseling of Youth in the Church, Paul B. Irwin. (Philadelphia: Fortress Press, 1975) $2.95. Offers guidance for developing counseling relationships with youth in the context of a caring community. (I)

Church Family Gatherings, Joe H. Leonard, Jr., ed. (Valley Forge: Judson Press, 1978) $4.95. Program resource for gatherings to include all age levels, including youth. (I)

Creative Youth Leadership, Janice Corbett. (Valley Forge: Judson Press, 1977) $4.25. A practical book for leaders seeking to understand youth, plan group activities, find and use resources, and develop "survival" skills. (M, E)

Explore series (Valley Forge: Judson Press) $6.95 (Volumes 1-3),

$11.95 (Volume 4). Four volumes of program resources for junior high groups. (M, E)

The Exuberant Years: A Guide for Junior High Leaders, Ginny W. Holderness. (Atlanta: John Knox Press, 1976) $6.50. A handbook to help workers with junior highs plan, develop, and carry out youth programming in the local church. (M)

Faith Shaping, Stephen D. Jones. (Valley Forge: Judson Press, 1980) $5.95. Nurturing the faith in youth is a continuing process—one that does not stop after his or her decision for Christ and church membership is made. This book explores the process and offers suggestions for the role of adults and the church. (M, E, I)

Free to Choose, Mary Adebonojo. (Valley Forge: Judson Press, 1980) $6.95. Creative programs and projects especially designed to meet the needs of black youth. (M)

How to Help a Friend, Paul Welter. (Wheaton: Tyndale House Publishers, 1978) $4.95. Practical helps for building helping relationships with others. (I)

New Games Book, and **More New Games and Playful Ideas,** both edited by Andrew Fluegelman (New York: Doubleday & Co., Inc., Dolphin, 1976, 1981) $6.95. Many, many games that encourage playing (over against winning), cooperation, self-competition, and players' creating their own rules. (M, E)

Reaching Youth Today: Heirs to the Whirlwind, Barbara Hargrove and Stephen D. Jones. (Valley Forge: Judson Press, 1983) $7.95. Explores the culture in which youth ministry takes place and looks at the rationale for and methods of youth evangelism. (M, E, I)

Respond series (Valley Forge: Judson Press) $5.95 (Volumes 1-5), $7.95 (Volume 6). Six volumes of program ideas, resources and leader tools for senior high groups. (M, E)

Retreat Handbook, Virgil Nelson and Lynn Nelson. (Valley Forge: Judson Press, 1976) $7.95. Chock-full of ideas, plans, and resources for retreats. (E)

Shaping the Church's Ministry with Youth, David M. Evans. (Valley Forge: Judson Press, 1977), rev. ed., $2.95. A revised, updated edition of a popular book calling for a reappraisal of youth ministry in church. (M, E, I)

Using Biblical Simulations, Volumes I & II, Donald E. Miller, Graydon F. Snyder and Robert W. Neff. (Valley Forge: Judson Press, 1973 and 1975) $7.95. Detailed descriptions of simulation games related to important biblical events. (E)

Values and Faith, Roland Larson and Doris Larson. (Minneapolis: Winston Press Inc., 1976) $5.95. A collection of value-clarifying exercises to be used for explorations of the Christian faith. (M, E)

Worship Celebrations for Youth, John Brown. (Valley Forge: Judson Press, 1980) $7.95. Resources for youth worship and gatherings. (M, E)

Youth Ministry: Sunday, Monday, and Every Day, John L. Carroll and Keith L. Ignatius. (Valley Forge: Judson Press, 1972) $2.95. A basic book for understanding the "whys" and "hows" of youth ministry. (M, E, I)

Youth Ministry: The Gospel and the People, Jan Chartier and Gabriel Fackre. (Valley Forge: Judson Press, 1979) $5.95. Foundational material in theology and adolescent development. (M, E, I)

Youth Ministry: The New Team Approach, Ginny W. Holderness. (Atlanta: John Knox Press, 1981) $9.95. A model to involve youth in the total life of the church. (M, E)